J 796.32364 ZADRA
Zadra, Dan.
Detroit Pistons /
33277000284609

J 796.32364 Z
Zadra, Dan

D0576157

136

.32364 Z
Dan.
J
796.    Pistons /     11.98
Z    00284609    Detroit Pistons

**CAMAS PUBLIC LIBRARY**
CAMAS, WASHINGTON

# DETROIT
## PISTONS

# DETROIT
PISTONS

DAN ZADRA

CREATIVE EDUCATION

CAMAS PUBLIC LIBRARY

**Photo Credit:** Creative Education would like to thank NBA photographer Ron Koch (New York City) for the color photography in this series.

Published by Creative Education Inc., 123 South Broad Street, Mankato, Minnesota 56001.

Copyright © 1989 by Creative Education, Inc. All rights reserved. No part of this book may be reproduced in any form without written permission from the publisher. Printed in the United States.

ISBN: 0-88682-203-3

**W**elcome to Detroit, Michigan. Affectionately known as the Motor City, Detroit is the world headquarters of General Motors, Chrysler Corporation, Ford Motor Company and the powerful United Auto Workers Union.

Antoine Cadillac founded a tiny French fort and trading village here in 1701. The Indian war chief, Pontiac, laid siege to the village in 1760. If only Cadillac and Pontiac were alive today. Imagine how amazed they would be to see their own names emblazoned on the sleek, modern automobiles that roll off the famous Detroit assembly lines.

Of course, if Detroit's avid basketball fans had their way, they might persuade local automakers to name a few new models after the men who have made the Detroit Pistons one of the top teams in the NBA. Such a fleet would surely include flashy turbo-charged models such as the Lanier, the Laimbeer, the Dantley, the Dumars, the Bing, the De-Busschere, the Thomas and the Tripucka.

Those are just a few of the exciting players who have proudly worn the Piston colors during the modern era of the NBA. But in the following pages, you will also meet several other interesting characters from an earlier period. These players and coaches may never be enshrined in the Hall of Fame, but they played a big role in forming the great Piston tradition. It is a tradition that stretches way back to the 1930s, an era when big league basketball was still in its infancy and still struggling for a place in the sun.

It was in 1937 that Fred Zollner of Fort Wayne, Indiana, decided to enter an amateur basketball team in a local industrial league. Zollner owned a large successful factory that made pistons for automobiles, so he just naturally named his team the Fort Wayne Pistons.

It seems Zollner was an inspirational fellow, reputed to be a great motivator. He was proud to say that not one of his employees had ever quit or been fired. His philosophy was simple: "Treat people like royalty, and they'll treat you like a king."

Like the employees in his factory, the players on Zollner's team worked together with great energy and enthusiasm. In no time at all, the Pistons easily outclassed every team in the league. "We rarely lost," said Zollner, "but that created a problem. Since we were playing against other factories, my team was making enemies for me, right and left."

**T**he solution was to drop out of the industrial league and step up to the professional ranks. In 1941, nine years before the NBA was even formed, the Fort Wayne Pistons officially joined the old National Basketball League. Once again they dominated, winning two straight titles in 1943-44 and 1944-45 with a close-knit team paced by the backcourt combination of Buddy Jeannette and Bobby McDermott.

In 1949, the NBL merged with the rival Basketball Association of America to form one unified league, today's National Basketball Association. The Fort Wayne Pistons were placed in the NBA's Central Division along with Minneapolis, Rochester, Chicago and St. Louis. This time, however, it was the Pistons who were outclassed. During their first five years in the league, Fort Wayne scrapped and battled but always ended each season in third or fourth place.

Meanwhile, however, Fred Zollner set a positive example for all the other NBA owners. Whether his team won or lost, he was determined to do everything possible to promote the game and the league to the American sports fan. He lent the league large sums of money to keep it afloat, allowed kids to attend Pistons games for free, and sponsored interesting clinics that explained the pro game to the fans.

Always the promoter, Zollner startled everyone by hiring an NBA referee, Charlie Eckman, to coach Fort Wayne in 1954-55. The fans were fascinated by the idea and flocked to Pistons games. But the other NBA coaches were insulted. They ridiculed Zollner and vowed to teach his "ref" a lesson.

■

*In only his second season in the NBA, Bob Lanier, averaged 25.7 points per game.*

Surprise! With a lineup that featured Max Zaslofsky, Andy Phillip, Frankie Brian, George Yardley, Larry Foust, Mel Hutchins and Bob Houbregs, coach Eckman led the Pistons all the way to the NBA championship series that season. Evidently, it was no fluke. The following season, 1955-56, Eckman's Pistons came back and won their second consecutive Western Division title and another trip to the playoffs.

The fans in little Fort Wayne rejoiced over their team's newfound success, but the celebration was short-lived. In 1957, Zollner sadly announced the truth. The population of Fort Wayne was simply too small to support a big league basketball club. With that, Zollner moved the team to the big, bustling city of Detroit.

As it turned out, the Pistons' first few years in the Motor City were sleepy ones, marked by one losing season after another. Gene Shue, their best guard, made the second team all-star roster in 1960-61. Bailey Howell, a Detroit forward, was one of the NBA's top rebounders that season. But it wasn't until rookie swingman Dave De-Busschere joined the club in 1962-63 that the action picked up.

DeBusschere, a local Detroit boy, was hailed throughout the league as the latest example of the NBA's increasing emphasis on defense. Like the Celtics' John Havlicek, the 6-foot-6 DeBusschere might score 20 points in a game and still leave the fans buzzing about his defensive steals and rebounds. He was one of the first NBA players to earn headlines through honest, hard-working attention to defense rather than offensive razzle-dazzle.

*High flyer: Gene Shue, a scrappy guard and a deadly shooter, was one of the Pistons' few stars in the early 1960s.*

In 1964, the Pistons made DeBusschere their player-coach. At 24, he was the youngest coach the league had ever had, and he did his best for four straight years to lead the Pistons out of the doldrums. Never once, however, did Detroit rise above fourth place in the Western Division. Their lone playoff appearance under DeBusschere came in 1967-68, a season that is probably best remembered as the year Pistons legend Dave Bing first came into his own.

Bing, an explosive shooting guard, had joined the Pistons in 1966 out of Syracuse University and had easily won Rookie of the Year honors. But no one in the league could've foreseen the heights to which he would soar just one year later. From the opening whistle of the 1967-68 season, Bing played with a ferocity and determination that startled even his own teammates. "I worry sometimes that Dave is packing his whole career into a single season," said DeBusschere.

By season's end, Bing had racked up an incredible 27.1 scoring average, becoming the first guard in twenty years to win the NBA scoring championship. Along the way, he had averaged 6.4 assists, fourth-best in the league behind Oscar Robertson, Len Wilkens and Wilt Chamberlain.

"You can't open up a man's chest and look at his heart," said Celtics coach Red Auerbach, "but I guarantee there's a big one beating in Bing. Give me one man like Dave Bing and I'll build a championship team around him."

That's exactly what the Pistons set out to do. With Bing anchoring the backcourt, Detroit

*Dave Bing*

# With Bing anchoring the backcourt, Detroit went in search of a big man.

went in search of a big man. They wanted a banger who could make up for the loss of Dave DeBusschere, who was traded away to the Knicks in the middle of the 1968-69 season. "We're getting hammered under the boards," admitted new head coach Dennis Butcher. "We'd all play better if we had a commanding presence on the front line."

The Pistons' search ended in 1970 at St. Bonaventure, a tiny college of 1,800 students tucked away in western New York. Playing center for the Bonaventure Indians was a remarkable 6-foot-11, 275-pound athlete by the name of Bob Lanier.

Oddly enough, the Pistons quickly discovered that the best part of their burly young r o o k i e ' s game was his velvety shooting touch. Most big players in those days had limited range. If a center did launch a shot from the top of the key, the ball clanged off the rim more often than it rippled the twine. But Lanier, the towering southpaw, had nights when he could lay outside and put up soft smooth jumpers or sweet little hookshots with unerring accuracy.

*Keith Herron*

**T**o help sharpen Lanier's rebounding and shot-blocking skills, the Pistons hired recently retired Bill Russell, the greatest defensive center in the history of the league, to be Bob's tutor. The result? Lanier led the Pistons to a 45-37 record in 1970-71. It was the first season since they landed in Detroit that the Pistons had achieved a winning record, but even better times lay ahead.

Though the Pistons slipped to a dismal 26-56 record in their injury-riddled 1971-72 campaign, new head coach Ray Scott quickly got them back on the winning trail. Scott, a colorful and popular sort of guy, was described by Lanier as a "player's dream come true." Scott refused to take credit for Piston victories. His favorite expression was, "A coach is only as good as his players."

Scott really got into the games. He paced the sidelines in a strange sort of quick time, looking like a fidgety actor in one of those old-time silent movies. "I've always gotten nervous like this," he explained. "When I was playing for the first time in a playoff game at Madison

## No longer would Detroit be considered the patsies of the Western Conference.

Square Garden, everyone else was acting real calm. I was so scared I put my shirt on backwards."

In 1973-74, Scott's Pistons came through with a scorching 52-30 regular season record. In the opening round of the playoffs, Detroit and Chicago battered each other in a seven-game series that riveted the attention of both cities. In the end, the Bulls won by a mere two points at home, but Scott and his Pistons had proved their point. No longer would Detroit be considered the patsies of the Western Conference. For his efforts Scott was voted the NBA Coach of the Year.

■
*The velvet touch: The Pistons snagged smooth-shooting giant Bob Lanier out of tiny St. Bonaventure college in 1970.*

**I**n 1974-75, ageless Dave Bing played his final year with the Pistons, finishing the season as the league's second-best assist maker with 610. "Now I want to go home and play out my final years with Washington," said Bing in his farewell to the Detroit fans. During his nine years in a Pistons uniform he had cracked the club's all-time top 10 list in 10 of 11 categories.

"How do you say good-bye to someone like that?" moaned coach Scott. But Scott himself would soon say adios. Without Bing, the Pistons sputtered during the first half of 1975-76 and Scott was replaced at midseason by unknown Herb Brown. It was not a popular move with the Pistons' followers.

"Herb, who?" wrote a disgruntled Detroit reporter, referring to Brown's undistinguished career. You see, Brown's previous two coaching positions had been with little C.W. Post College and with the Israel Sabras in the European Professional Basketball League. To make matters worse, rumor had it that Brown and the players didn't hit it off too well in their first few meetings. The players complained about his cranky disposition and his tough New York accent.

"I just don't like the way he sounds when he's criticizing me," complained Lanier. "What he's saying may be right, but sometimes I just can't listen."

■
*Bob Lanier (left) sneaks his big left hand in for a steal against the Kings.*

**I**n Brown's first full season at the helm, 1976-77, the Pistons played quite well, finishing at 44-38. Still, it seemed at times as if the ship was sinking. The season was more like a soap opera than anything else. The players would gripe about Brown; then Brown would gripe about the players. Local newspapers recorded every spat. It was sad to see top pros such as Kevin Porter, Chris Ford, Eric Money and Bob Lanier openly squabble with their coach.

Obviously, some changes were in order. Halfway through the 1977-78 season the Pistons fired Brown and let general manager Bob Kauffman handle the rest of the season before hiring Dick Vitale. No help. Vitale was a newcomer to the pro ranks and his inexperience showed. The Pistons struggled to win a mere 30 games in 1978-79. One of the season's few highlights was provided by Lanier who scored 10 points and blocked a key shot in the All-Star game. That was Bob's final All-Star appearance as a Detroit Piston.

The following year, Lanier was traded to the Milwaukee Bucks. Twelve games into the season, the Pistons fired Dick Vitale and hired Richie Adubato. Poor Richie. He inherited a discouraged group of mediocre players who felt lost without Lanier at center. It was no great surprise when Detroit sagged to a 16-66 record in 1979-80, followed by a 21-61 mark in 1980-81. The Pistons had lost their spark, but then along came the 1981 college draft.

"The Pistons will benefit from the trading and drafting policies of general manager Jack McCloskey, as well as the coaching of Scotty Robertson," predicted an analyst for the *NBA Guide*. It was a pretty safe prediction. You see, Detroit had just snagged Isiah Thomas and Kelly Tripucka in the college draft.

**T**he two young rookies were as different from each other as night and day. Barely 20 years old, Thomas was a 6-foot-1, 185-pound guard who hailed from a tough black ghetto in Chicago. Tripucka was a 6-foot-6, 220-pound forward who had grown up in a posh white suburb of New Jersey. Thrown together on the same team, the two would soon be hailed as twin saviors in the Motor City.

The first thing everyone noticed about Thomas was his toothy grin which stretched from ear to ear. "I have a lot to smile about," he softly told the Detroit reporters. "I realize how lucky I am."

**Thrown together on the same team, the two would soon be hailed as twin saviors in the Motor City.**

**T**homas was one of nine children in a very poor family. He recalled that the cupboard was often empty and that life on the streets of Chicago's West Side wasn't much fun.

"There were people who got shot and stabbed and all that stuff," said Isiah. "I appreciate it even more now. Take something like shoes. You take care of them better because when you were young and got a pair, they had to last for a year or two. Or three meals a day. I know everybody doesn't get that."

When Isiah was four, his father left the family. His mother struggled to make ends meet, relying on leftovers discarded by the cafeteria where she worked. Isiah and his mom became very close. "I was kind of like Isiah's first coach," she told a Detroit reporter. "I'd always talk to him and wherever I went, he went. We walked and talked many a day together when he was younger. He probably didn't understand what I was saying, but he looked up at me like he did."

Isiah understood, all right. He appreciated what his mother was doing for him and promised to steer clear of the street scene. By the time he entered St. Joseph's High School, basketball had become his main outlet. He led St. Joseph's to a 73-15 record over three years. After high school Isiah went on to spark the Indiana Hoosiers to the NCAA championship in his sophomore year of college. Then he shocked the Indiana fans by announcing that he intended to quit college and play in the NBA.

"It was the security I needed for me, my family and the family I intend to start someday," Isiah explained. "I know the value of a degree, but I will go back to school someday. Right now, my mother and my family come first."

*Adrian Dantley drives past an unidentified Net defender.*

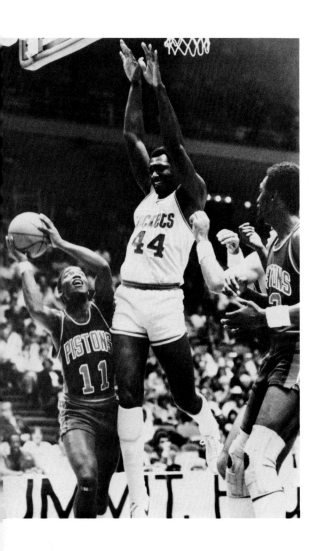

*Isiah Thomas*

**E**arly in the 1981-82 season it appeared that Isiah would be the runaway winner of the NBA's Rookie of the Year award. He was scoring almost at will and winning lots of fans with his friendly smile. After watching Isiah dismantle the Milwaukee Bucks' defense one evening, the Pistons' Will Robinson said in tribute: "I believe God made people to perform certain arts. Frank Sinatra was made to sing, Jesse Owens was made to run and Isiah Thomas was made to play basketball."

Meanwhile, however, Kelly Tripucka was making his own bid for stardom. Night after night, the former Notre Dame standout was everywhere all at once, snagging rebounds, diving for loose balls and piling up the points.

"Kelly's got a heart as big as Dallas," marvelled coach Robertson the night Tripucka burned Julius Erving and the Philadelphia 76ers for 38 points. "He reminds me of John Havlicek, the way he just out-desires

## Meanwhile, Kelly Tripucka was making his own bid for stardom.

everyone. I don't think Kelly thinks of himself as a rookie. Give him the ball and he'll challenge anybody."

By season's end, Tripucka had a 21.6 scoring average, good enough to qualify as runner-up to New Jersey's Buck Williams in Rookie of the Year balloting. Isiah had averaged 17 points and 7.8 assists. And Detroit had improved its record by 18 games over the year before, finishing 39-43 and inspiring this comment by a veteran NBA reporter:

"So dynamic were the resurrected Pistons that it was difficult for people who had enjoyed their aggressive style to understand how they missed the playoffs. The Pistons are unmistakably a team on the rise."

**U**nfortunately, Kelly Tripucka missed 24 games because of injury in 1982-83. Isiah Thomas did his best to take up the slack, becoming one of only four players in the NBA to finish in the top 10 in three categories: assists, steals and three-pointers. And Pistons center Bill Laimbeer did his part by vacuuming 12.1 rebounds per game, third best in the league. Still, the Pistons' record actually fell by a couple of games to 37-45, and that cost coach Robertson his job.

Quickly, the Pistons went in search of Robertson's replacement. The fans held their breath as general manager Jack McCloskey announced the name of the club's new leader. "The Pistons have selected Chuck Daly as our new head coach," said McCloskey. Detroit's fortunes were about to take a giant turn for the better.

*Kelly Tripucka*

Daly, a 52-year-old alumnus of Pennsylvania's Bloomsburg University, quickly made friends with the players, the fans and the Detroit media. He had a gift of gab, a good sense of humor and a gee-whiz way of discussing the game. "Gosh," he told the press, "I'm not sure our players realize just how good they really are. I guess maybe my first job is to help them see that they belong with the best."

Consistency was one of Daly's favorite themes. "This club has never had back-to-back winning seasons," he explained. "If the players can learn to understand their roles better, we'll begin to win on a consistent basis. Then we'll just hope to build each year on our past success."

**W**ith Daly at the helm the Pistons reeled off three consecutive winning seasons, including three straight trips to the NBA playoffs. Their record in 1983-84 was 49-33, followed by two identical 46-36 marks. The roles of the key players in all three seasons seemed clear. "The Pistons utilized the magical speed of guard Isiah Thomas, the drive of forward Kelly Tripucka and the tenacity of center Bill Laimbeer to frustrate opponents and pack the spacious Pontiac Silverdome with record crowds," wrote a *Sporting News* analyst.

## "Gosh," he told the press, "I'm not sure our players realize just how good they really are."

*Kent Benson (54) battles for a rebound during a game with the New Jersey Nets.*

**A**s far as coach Daly was concerned, however, that was just the warm-up. After the Pistons were eliminated by the Atlanta Hawks in the first round of the 1985-86 playoffs, Daly sent an extraordinarily confident message of assurance to the fans. "I hope you won't get discouraged," he said. "We are going to accomplish something this franchise has never had, an NBA championship."

It was exciting stuff, made even more exciting by the announcement of a new addition to the Pistons lineup. In a bold stroke, general manager Jack McCloskey engineered a trade that sent Detroit forwards Kelly Tripucka and Kent Benson to the Utah Jazz in exchange for veteran forward Adrian "A.D." Dantley. At 6-foot-5, Dantley was a deadly shooter and an absolute master of the inside move.

"Once A.D. gets a defender on his hip," wrote an analyst for *Dick Vitale's Basketball*, "he's either putting

## Dantley was a deadly shooter and an absolute master of the inside move.

two in the books or taking a trip to the line. His clever offense can literally take over a game."

When the Pistons went 3-6 to start the 1986-87 season, the rumors flew that Thomas and Dantley had clashed egos and that the Pistons were a team divided. As the season wore on, however, coach Daly insisted that his players had finally settled happily into their respective roles.

*Detroit center Kent Benson (left) stuffs one past Pacers forward Mike Bantom in 1981 action.*

CAMAS PUBLIC LIBRARY

**E**veryone knows that Isiah is our floor general," said Daly. "He gets everyone involved in the offense, which results in a very unselfish basketball team. Dantley is a pro's pro. Our players call him "The Teacher" because he shows everyone how to win by his example, both on and off the court. And Bill Laimbeer is another veteran who plays hard every night, and that makes the other players do the same."

Urged on by capacity crowds in the Silverdome, the Pistons raced to the most successful season in the history of the franchise up to that point, winning 52 games and peaking just in time for the '87 playoffs. After eliminating both Washington and Atlanta, the Pistons had a classic showdown with the Celtics in the Eastern Conference finals.

"It was the most intense battle I have ever been involved in," said coach Daly of a series that saw the Pistons push the Celtics to seven games. An errant pass by Isiah Thomas in the final seconds of Game 5 was intercepted by Larry Bird who fed Dennis Johnson for the game-winner. Otherwise, the Pistons would've possibly met the Lakers for the NBA championship.

A few weeks later Coach Daly met with a writer for the *NBA Yearbook* and cited the Pistons' "superior depth" as a cause for optimism in 1987-88. Beyond Thomas, Dantley and Laimbeer, Detroit boasted first and second-line strength at every position.

Vinnie Johnson, a dangerous 6-foot-2 shooting guard, was one of the league's top sixth men. Third-year guard Joe Dumars was a savvy defender and a key to Daly's fast break.

■

*The Iron Man: Bill Laimbeer played in 646 consecutive regular season games through 1986-87, a new club record.*

**I**n the forward rotation, the Pistons could go with super-fast John Salley and Dennis Rodman or insert bruiser Rick Mahorn. In addition, Detroit had recently picked up 7-foot forward/center William Bedford from the Phoenix Suns and high-scoring guard Freddie Banks from the college draft.

The stage was set. As brilliant as the Pistons had been in 1987, they were even better in 1988. They played together with a fierce commando style described by Laimbeer as "ask no quarter, take no prisoners."

"We have to play this way if we expect to achieve our goals this year," said Daly. "We get a lot of ridicule and harrassment from opposing fans because we play so intensely. But they have to understand that we can't sneak up on anyone anymore. Everyone in the league is gunning for us now."

When the smoke had cleared, the Pistons stood atop the Central Divison with a franchise best 54-28 record. In the first round of the 1988 playoffs, they came from behind to zap the Bullets in five games, 3-2. Against Chicago in the second round, the Pistons did what few other teams in the league had been able to do. They virtually grounded the Bulls' high-flying Michael "Air" Jordan and easily won the series, 4-1.

■

*The acquistion of Adrian "A.D." Dantley from the Utah Jazz in 1986 made the Pistons a certain playoff contender.*

**N**ow, for the second straight year, the Pistons met the Celtics for the Eastern Conference championship. After four games the series was tied and Boston still had the homecourt advantage. But in Game 5 the Pistons shocked the Celtics by defeating them on the legendary parquet floor of Boston Garden and then won the series in Game 6 before a wildly cheering crowd at the Pontiac Silverdome. Finally, the Pistons were bound for the NBA Finals.

"We're about as ready as ready can be," said Isiah Thomas as the Pistons boarded a plane bound for Los Angeles, home of the Western Conference champion Lakers. "We all know what our mission is."

But the Lakers were on a mission, too. After winning the NBA title in 1987, their coach, Pat Riley, had blurted a brash promise. "I guarantee the Lakers will repeat as champions in 1988," he had said. Could the Pistons make him eat his words?

---

## Finally, the Pistons were bound for the NBA Finals.

---

During the final hours leading up to the first game, the series was hyped in the media as an offensive showdown. Isiah Thomas vs. Magic Johnson. Adrian Dantley vs. James Worthy. Surely, predicted the experts, the fans would be treated to fast breaks, dazzling moves and high scores.

*Team leader Isiah Thomas elevated the Pistons into the playoffs for five straight seasons, 1984-88.*

Instead, the Pistons set the tone for the series by defeating the Lakers at home in Game 1 with a gritty style of defense that allowed Los Angeles to score just 93 points. It was the first time in 21 playoff games that the Lakers had been held below 100 points. "It's simple," shrugged Isiah after the game. "The best defense is going to win this series."

The Lakers won the next two games, but the Pistons responded with two straight wins of their own. Their victory in Game 5 came in the Silverdome and was witnessed by more than 41,000 fans, the largest playoff crowd in NBA history.

Despite a sprained back and ankle, Isiah Thomas managed to score 43 points in Game 6, but the Lakers held on to send the series into the seventh and deciding game. By now, Isiah was limping like a wounded soldier and that gave the Lakers the winning edge. With seven minutes to go, Los Angeles had built a gaping 15-point lead. Detroit's Joe Dumars and Vinnie Johnson led a miraculous 17-4 run that brought the Pistons within one point with six seconds remaining. But the Lakers' A.C. Green sank a layup to give Los Angeles a 108-105 triumph.

What a series it had been. Los Angeles had fulfilled Pat Riley's promise by becoming the first NBA team in 19 years to repeat as champions. And the Pistons? How would *they* react to a drama that had left them vanquished after coming so tantalizingly close to earning the first NBA title in the club's 48-year history in the league?

Asked to sum up his teammates' attitude about the loss, Bill Laimbeer used one word: "Defiant." He explained that each year under coach Daly the Pistons had come closer and closer to their dream, the NBA title.

"Do you think we're going to stop now?" he asked incredulously. "This is the NBA. You've got to hammer and hammer and hammer over the years, and eventually your time will come. If you bash on that door long enough, it will fall down."

■